The Quiet Child

ஐ Poems ლ

Darlene C Alvarez

The Quiet Child – Poems. © 2007 by Darlene C Alvarez
All rights reserved. No part of this book may be used or reproduced in any manner whatsoever without written permission except in the case of brief quotations embodied in critical articles or reviews.

Front cover photograph/Book layout by Darlene C Alvarez
Author photograph by José A Alvarez

ISBN 978-0-6151-5237-0

Printed in the United States of America

The Quiet Child

᙭ Poems ᙮

For José and Jennifer,

my laughter and sunshine

Acknowledgments

As I share my words with the world, I want to express much gratitude for *your* words:

-of **Love** and **Encouragement**
(from my Mom, M. Clar;
my Brother, D. Cagampan; my Family)

-of **Constructive Criticism**
(from my Teachers: A. Puretz; E. Barranco;
M. Fong; M. Jackson; E. Constable)

-of **Perseverance**, **Eloquence** and **Simplicity**
(from C. Hart, through the gift of your music)

-of **Acceptance**
(from Editors who featured my poems in
various publications)

You made me believe in myself – you're fabulous and I thank you!

-dca

Contents

#1 Fan 17

10,000 Years 18

A Bar to Raise 20

Allaying Hubby Fears 21

Almorranas 23

Angel Cursing at Me 24

Blasé 25

Closet Elitist 27

Clubbings 28

Come Running 29

Contradiction 31

Cork! 32

Déjà vu 33

Dense 34

Depiction 35

Deranged, but not derailed 36

Docile Wife 37

Drawers 39

Eat My Young 41

Epine chérie 42

Evasion 44

Extraction 45

Filtered 46

Finger 47

Fix your cats! 48

Foreigner Born Here 50

Forgiving Myself 51

Friends on a Train 52

Funnel 53

Gone 54

Hairs 55

Harassment 56

hillcrest 58

Home Is Wherever You Are 60

Hornball 62

How Does A Cloud Taste? 63

If You Love Someone 65

I Hear Him in the Words I Don't Speak 66

Ils me manquent 68

In My Puffy Parka 69

Isang puso 71

It Is Time 72

It'll Be Better In A Second 74

It's Not Me, It's You 76

I Wish I Could Tell You 78

Joy To My World 79

Krush 80

Las Vegas Haiku (5) 82

Last Warm Breeze of Summer 83

Looking Out Kleiber's Window 85

Look, Ma, we're married 86

Lover on Death Row 87

Maybe it was decaf? 89

Montluçon, le 27-28 août 1995 90

Musings of the Sunlight-Deprived 92

My Life as a Monk 93

Oh When I Remember 95

Paper Dolls 96

Paris *encore* 97

Passenger 99

Peace o'Paper (POP) 101

Poke Her Face 102

Preservation 104

Prière du chat 106

Puedo amar 108

Quiero dormir ahora 109

Red-Light Runner 110

Roller Skates 113

Routine 115

Salope ivrée 117

Settling 118

Silent Lamb 119

Split Ends 120

Spoiled 122

Step 123

Still Questioning 124

Suspend-Her 126

Synthetic Happy Place 127

Take Back The Wheel 129

Taken For Granted 130

Tea Leaves 133

The Carousel (bittersweet '01) 134

The Collector 136

The Love Dispenser 138

Then and Now 141

The Sister I Never Had 143

The Slumber He Seeks 145

Tongue alive 146

Too Much on my Template 147

Tough As Nails 148

Trust me, sweetie 149

Two Words 150

Une amie qui s'appelait Rose 151

Unsentimental 153

Valentine 155

Walking Around Squinting 156

Who askew? 157

Winner 158

Wisdom 159

You Said To Me 160

You think? 162

#1 Fan

When you're rocking her to sleep

Tears well up in your eyes

You need to look no further

As your #1 fan is

Dreaming to your lullabies

10,000 Years

As I sit here in a corner
Of the cubby-hole of a room I have
I'm writing under the dim glare of the lamp
Powering a 60-watt bulb

I contemplate a little
Then I ponder a lot
I am but a booger
In this universe!

They say if you do something
you're not happy with
Let it go
It won't matter 10,000 years from now
But if you do something good for all
10,000 years from now
Will they know who to properly credit?

So either way, what we do or not
Will have no bearing, good or not

Hmmm. I think I'll live for today.

Like someone great first suggested some

10,000 years ago.

A Bar to Raise

You're not supposed to be happy
The ugly bitch said
You're not supposed to laugh or smile
But be miserable instead

You're not supposed to be successful
The mediocre one declared
You're not supposed to have and be all that
No one motivated me, no one cared

You're not supposed to be rich
Said the stupid derelict
You're not supposed to have such freedom
Just take whatever and not have your pick

Why people like you exist
I stop to ask myself and wonder
It's to provide a bar to raise -
I hope I don't fall under

Allaying Hubby Fears

In the past, I'd asked for not much
And that was all I got
      Who said happiness can't be bought?

All I ask of you
Is a little box in powder-blue
Wrapped in a silky ribbon all around
A diamond in a princess cut
      Wait – I see I've made you frown!

You fear I'll spend all your money
That I won't let you hang with your boys
That one day the haze of love will pass
That everything I do just annoys –

You think, "Damn, I'll never eat buffet again!
I'm stuck at the same restaurant!"
"For the rest of my life, dealing with your
      crazy family
Dodging my 'favorite' neurotic aunt"

You fear you'll never again see me in
>high heels and short skirts

That I'll permanently replace my wardrobe
>with jeans and sweats

You fear my inconsiderate extravagance
>will send us

Spiraling downwards into inescapable debt

Congratulations, you're the lucky one
I don't want to repeat asking for nothing
Then 100 years later thinking
"Is that all I get?"

But don't get me wrong, darling
As this is all in fun
Love is all that matters
When it comes to what I want
You're the only one.

Almorranas

My poor, poor sphincter's sore
Waging an all-out war
My gut and stuff didn't like what I ate
Forget digestion it came out straight

Angel Cursing at Me

Somewhere my angel is cursing me out
       for having doubt
That she wasn't there for me that night
Did she sleep at the wheel
Like the driver who hit us

My angel calls me an ingrate, yelling
"you're alive aren't you?
What more are you asking for?"

No, wait
That was my lawyer

Blasé

Unimpressed by the shimmering Porsche
You sidled up against
'cause you can't afford to appear that you
Can't afford it

I'm wearing a cardigan
But it looks like a sweater to you
There's nothing said
You've never heard before
No joke funny
The second time around

In awe of very little
Moved by even less
You have eyes of jade -
You're no fun!

How are we supposed to discover together?
Sometimes I want to shake you like a leaf
To have the righteousness fall out

To pluck your feathers
So you have nothing to cock about

Actually I did once
Nothing came out
So you scoff and turn your nose up
Not because you're above that

It's to disguise your ignorance of it
You can't afford to appear that you
Can't afford
To lose face

That's all you have.

Closet Elitist

The sky used to be the minimum

Negativity was a foreign concept

Ambition the driving force

The reason to live

Somehow I've slipped on the average shoes

As I traipse along mediocre lane…

My uneasiness and discomfort

Only show that I don't belong here

That I need to regain my bearings

To get back on track

Clubbings

Haphazard stares

Deliberately choose me

Random access to countless ass

Hands running wild and free

Across seemingly unchartered prairies

Untouched by man

Butt if things go well…change is good!

Hedonistic urges take over

Hard-headedness brings me back there

As a fortuitous encounter I hope for

Is strategically executed

Come Running

You attract trouble like shit attracts the flies
Chaos follows you 'round like a nympho
      after guys

You're the captivated audience for countless
      dramas
You come running with your first-aid kit to
      repair traumas

But who comes running when your nose is
      bleeding
Who comes to lend a hand when your spirit's
      needing

A kind word, a pat on the back

It's not your duty oh so eager to please
It's not your job to change things
      a hundred-eighty degrees
You're ready for each situation with your

safety net
But a little appreciation you have not seen yet

But who comes running when you're
    under a cloud
Who comes rushing to you when you're
    feeling too proud

For a hug, or to ask for help

Hey, buddy, could you use a hand
Turn to me and I'll understand

So who'll come running when your heart is
    breaking
Who'll come with some ice cream and doesn't
    mind sharing

I am here, could you take some please?

Contradiction

Help me be self-reliant

Hold my hand while I try to let you go

I depend on your weakness

To assert my strength

I will not put up with your intolerance

As if I care what you think

Is that OK with you?

Take me as I am – dammit!

The way you want me to be.

Cork!

You say it was my flatulence

That caused major turbulence

For it you lacked the tolerance

In my defense

I don't see the relevance

Hence,

I demand some recompense

That you minimize its influence

It makes no sense

Would it have been better had I been tense

Or had some reticence?

I've since made improvements

Déjà vu

She suddenly
Called off
Her engagement, so I'm told, rather
Abruptly, it's like
Déjà vu to get the gossip, I'm
Ecstatic not to be the only one to go through
    this
No offers of sympathy nor
Friendship from me, though now she and I can
    better
Relate – the spoiled brat who has
Everything suddenly does not
Unless he dumped her, in which case, I can't
    relate, sister!
Delighted in knowing she'll recover either way
Ephemeral bliss, too, shall pass.

Dense

Do my diminutive ears
Scream speak to me
Do my glazed over eyes
Invite elaborate detail
Do my stifled yawn and
Quivering lips
Suggest you go on
Do my snores
Provide harmony to your voice
Do my headphones
Recommend you just speak louder
"shut up!" I request
"How rude of you," you say
"to interrupt me mid-sentence!"
Do my crossed arms
Show heightened interest
Do my exasperated sighs
Mean I'm basking in the intrigue
Do my diminutive ears
Scream!

Depiction

(Previously published in Northern Exposure, 2005)

Whether fiery sunbeams naturally target
Or a heating unit is propped up nearby
The snow really melts
      A picture captures that truth

Put little girls in pearls and high heels
Little boys in suits bearing flowers
They look really grown
      A picture captures their youth

They make you say cheese to produce a smile
As they immortalize this memory
You look really happy
      So a picture captures this bliss

You toil and travail then you reach the summit
Red ribbon rips across your chest
You are so victorious
      But a picture captures, "is that all there is?"

Deranged, but not derailed

I used to think I was the only sane one left
That everyone else should be in the bin
But after a minor perspective adjustment
Maybe they're OK and I should check in

Docile Wife

I envisage my future:
Me, opening the door
For his business cohorts
I am standing there
Wearing a single-strand pearl necklace
      and a *Chanel* outfit
Like the knock-off that hangs in my closet now

Around the dining table
Coffee, anyone?   I ask as the meal,
Served on the finest china, of course, ends
He talks and cracks jokes
As an approving nod, smile, and giggle
From his right encourage him on

My laugh is interrupted
As I'm complimented on my 'do
      and that same *Chanel* outfit

But all I can say is:

Everyone at my PTA meetings

Has the same outfit and matching *Louboutins*

Though my shrink says

I should experiment with color

I only refrain from wearing this

At my AA meetings

Because it's really rather too formal…

But, thank you.

Drawers

The kitten heel of my shoe
Went thump! against the ceiling
Now it's marred for good
I plop onto the couch
Rolling my stockings down
Until they look like a pair of
Nylon onion rings
On the floor
The pungent scent released
Has me hankering for some
Fish and chips
From that place on A and 2nd Streets
With the red and white awning
Taking a breather, I sit back
Inhale and release
The putrid scent
Reminds me of the peppered pastrami
    sandwich
I had for lunch at that place on Pine Street
I pull my barrette off

As my chestnut brown #245 split-ended mane
    tumbles free
Of fried tilapia, cigarette smoke and ammonia
    from the kitty's pee
Smells the scum underneath my nails
Clearly built-up from the day before yesterday
When I showered last
Stuff collects in my drawers
Suddenly I understand his attraction
To the lingerie stores
The intoxicating scent is perverse and
    should be banned
Release the shady, seedy little man!

Eat My Young

Silky strands of French roast coffee
      Unruly crown
Ocular chestnuts
      Winkers
Red strawberries
      Smilers
Chicken drummettes
      Huggers
Ham hocks
      Kickers
Apricots
      Tickle spot
Pan de sal
      Diaper holders
Unwrinkled raisins
      Mid-day snacks

Epine chérie

Comme une épine

Tu as fait de la peine à moi

Comme une épine

Tu as protégé la fleur

Comme une épine

Tu m'as touché profondément

Comme une épine

Tu as fait mon sang à couler

Comme une épine

Vous êtes toujours trop nombreux

Mais, tu étais le seul que j'ai voulu

Alors, j'ai te cueilli

Mais, tu m'as piqué plutôt

Comme une épine

Je te retirerai de moi

Et lécherai mes blessures

Comme une épine

Tu laisseras une cicatrice

Et je la regarderai

En pensant de toi

Car c'est tout que j'ai

Comme quelqu'un

Sans une épine.

Evasion

Il n'est qu'une évasion pour moi
La pensée de lui m'aider à oublier
Tous ce qui m'inquiéter
Et il y a beaucoup de choses
Qui flottent dans ma tête
Il représent la liberté de tous
Ce qui sont sensibles
Alors, je cherche mon abri dans lui
Au moins, dans la pensée de lui.

Extraction

When I think back

I think how sad

I am I was back

Then I think bad

Thoughts and get mad

At how I can't go back

Make things good

Luck is what you make

It sucks that I only know

That now that I am older

Than I was yesterday

When I had my wisdom teeth

Take 'em out I said I think

They don't work anyway

Until you take 'em out

Wisdom comes when you

Realize you don't

Need 'em after all

Filtered

His cheeks shine with the clear gloss of tears
Like a badge of honor for his ordeal
His mouth is stretched from ear to ear
But it's no grin
As he whimpers and groans
His ivory teeth gleam against his ebony skin
Much like they did weeks before
When he and some friends went swimming in
    a dark, murky pond
He took care not to swallow for his mother
    had warned him
Still his ears got waterlogged and droplets
    seeped into his wide nose
He recalls wailing in joy as he emerged,
    refreshed
He is making a noise again as he writhes in the
Excruciating sensation
As they extract the serpentine consequence

Finger

If I'd had this rock on my finger then
It would've served as a reminder that
His thigh was off limits
If I'd had this rock on my finger then
It would've served as a reminder that
I should let go when he holds my hand
If I'd had this rock on my finger then
It would've blinded me
As I touched his face
If I'd had this rock on my finger then
It would've served as a reminder that
I should get up off his chest
If I'd had this rock then
I would have had a reminder
This symbol of your love for me
If I'd had this rock then
I'd have shown it to him -
My finger.

Fix your cats!

Of the exactly 7 or 8 kittens
The one named Precious is out in the cold
While the exactly 6 or 7, I think
Are scattered about town
Pooping in their self-cleaning litter boxes
Sleeping in their warm and fuzzy
Fleece-lined kitty beds

The one named Precious is without a home
While the exactly 5 or so others
Feast on fancy fare
Play with feathers and strings of bells
Scratch on fleece-covered posts

The one named Precious
I only hope can tell fresh water
From anti-freeze run-off
A catnip-filled toy
From a diseased mouse
A parked car

From an 18-wheeler coming at full speed

The one so precious
I hope another can see, too
And can take him inside
Then love him better than I do.

Foreigner Born Here

I feel a foreigner born here

More than your ambition

I'm drawn to your plight

I admire your courage to pursue

I envy your freedom to choose

Your accent seems heavy

Only because of

The weight of the words of your story

I'm enthralled by it

Your speech is broken but your spirit is not

That is what I'm hearing

That is why I understand

I'm not listening with my ears

But with my heart and my own spirit

Still in search of a home

Forgiving Myself

I'm paying the toll
For the bridge
I crossed
Even though it –
I was going the wrong way

I'm carrying memories
Of a person
I crossed
I'm feeling remorse for a
Past transgression

Which in spite of itself
Will never be met
With regret.

Friends on a Train

The metal scratching along the rails
The lights flashing on and off
The cramped cabin holding eight
I can't breathe
My head laying on a pillow you offered
I lose myself in comfort
Forgetting about how you managed through
      the night
I think we're here, you whispered
Sitting up I look out the window
Lamplights still dotting the midnight blue
      horizon
You rise and walk away to your private corner
Arms outstretched the length of the window
Staring blankly out as the trees whiz on by

Funnel

Walls shrinking, egos expanding
Something will be compromised
Cramped/stifled/suffocated/invaded/
    intruded upon
Like each passing day
Closer to the end
Final move-in day
When you check out
Put on the shelf
Oh unsuspecting harbor of doom
Portable, stackable, convalescent home
Of dreams and things
Where youth and useful matter
All else left neglected
To yellow, fade, be forgotten
Your legacy the delectable stench
Permeating in the air
Chain coming full circle
As another generation of amoebae goes on

Gone

Like the kindergarten picture

You cannot take now

Like the milk you cannot drink

From the butcher's cow

Like my taut skin and supple body

Splendid performance

Show's over, take your bow

Like the few moments

You took to read up 'til now

Hairs

The hairs on my arms

Are short, dark, sparse and wiry

Like the ones down there

Harassment

Them, you and I we congregate
But of all of them
You make me hyperventilate
Can't ask you repeatedly for a date
I think you and I should fornicate
But safe not stupid and not procreate
No strings attached, let's just recreate
If you are the subject, allow me to predicate
Our sentence will read more love less hate
My revved up desires will have to wait
      Troublesome disruptive discord
      Is not what I want to create
Forgive me as I'm captivated by
      your self-assured gait
Tight ass and cavernous cleavage the
      unreachable bait
As I fantasize about the fusion of pulsating
      warm human flesh
Uncontrollably I salivate

Them, you and I we congregate

By the water cooler, I smile and lie

I say it's what I ate

To abide by *Code* and maintain integrity

From you I must reluctantly separate

hillcrest

"If anyone asks, I'll say my name is
Margarita," my mother said,
with cigarette and almost-empty lighter
in hand.

The stairwell was orange-red, like papaya
meat.

Old, stuck-on gum, spit out probably by the
one who peed there, dotted the concrete steps.

I kept track of the days on a calendar page I
had made from a sheet of wide-ruled binder
paper. I hung it on the wall sideways, with the
3 holes running along the top.

Years later, my brother's friend asked, "You
used to live there, didn't you?" as we passed
by hillcrest. My brother's eyes bulged out -
Oh, no, he di'nt just ask me that!

The Quiet Child

Years later still, while driving his slick, new, limited-edition sports car, my brother passed by an old white van. He turned to his friend, "You used to live in there, didn't you?"

No, he didn't -
really ask him, that is.

Home Is Wherever You Are

Home is wherever you are
You awaken the clumsy giant
You're the cat who's caught my tongue
You inspire me, you make me smile
Sweet as the melody the bluebird sung

Hand in hand we travel along the long road
Though with you it is not daunting
Heart to heart we offer ourselves to each other
Sharing, revealing, opening, embracing
The other's demons that once were haunting

Your love is the elixir to cure all my raw,
blistering wounds
In an instant, I am renewed

Your hug, your kiss
The way you accept me, like this
Is all I've ever wanted

I've always said,

"Home is wherever you are"

For this house shall never be haunted

Hornball

Beads of sweat form in my cleavage
And as they roll down
I giggle 'cause they tickle
My shirt needs to be peeled off
A second skin – I prefer you
It's been so long
I'd settle for a flash right about now
But unless it's you underneath that trench coat
I will be disappointed.

Like a snowman
I walked into my greenhouse apartment
What to do now with the runoff…
Buckets, baby
Can only hold a second's worth
Open up your reservoir
I have so much to give you
Help me to contain myself
Only you can
Careful, it's slick in the gutters.

How Does A Cloud Taste?

How does a cloud taste?
What would it feel like as it hit your face?
Would a puff of it get stuck in my hair?

"Are you crying?"
No, I've got some cloud in my eye.

Could I bottle it up?
I'd keep it in a jar on my kitchen counter.
"No cloud before dinner or it'll ruin your
      appetite."

Could it lift me up when I feel low?
I just want to leave you all
Down here for a minute
"Legalize clouds, man."

Could it carry me away
Or would I fall through?

Would it blur my vision
Or could I see through?

Swimming in the sky
With a cloud as a lifesaver
I reach and I soar
I crash into a hot air balloon

It asked me, "Are you happy?"

Before I knew it, the gears lowered
The cloud came in for a smooth landing
The cloud did fill me up
But I still don't know
What it tastes like.

If You Love Someone

The picture I have in my mind

Is of you smiling

It's incredibly endearing

How you let your vulnerabilities show

Only to me

While the rest of the world

Shake in their boots because

You're so strong

But you crawl into my lap

At the end of the day

You tell me you're still searching

You want me to help you find

So now I feel beautiful and powerful

     in my own way

How you trust me! You know you can

In my arms, I'll cradle your head

You've used it all day

I'll hold your hand to guide you -

Help you find your way

I Hear Him in the Words I Don't Speak

Now that father's gone
    I see
How very much alive
    He is

I see it
    In my reflection
    In my wide nose
    In my round brown eyes
    In the dimple on my cheek
I even hear him
    In the words I don't speak

I inherited his appeasing way -
Rather than have a showdown
Opting instead to walk away

I realize it wasn't that he didn't care
Maybe it's because he cared too much?
Just too proud to let it show

For fear of ridicule

Of being mistaken for weakness

…guess I'll never truly know.

Ils me manquent

A l'avance je n'avais pas assez de la confiance
En moi et en mon aptitude
Donc, je m'abstenais d'écrire en français
    encore,
Jusqu'à ce moment

C'est amusant pour moi comment je peux
    narguer
A ma sentimentalité, comme si c'était une loi
Rien ont changé – je cour vers à cette-ville-là
Où tant des belles images vivent
La chose nouvelle est la façon dont je les vois
J'accepte finalement qu'elles soient passées
Avec ma tête, je pense d'eux
C'est comme si mon cœur s'est endurcit

In My Puffy Parka

Back when Paula and Janet were still friends
They danced across the pink television screen
What have you done for me lately?

I sat hunched-back, as usual, on the foot
    of the bed
In my puffy gray and white parka
Way before they were cool and all the rage

His scruffy pathetic excuse for a beard
Grew in spots
Where pus-filled, blistering acne missed

I scooted to my left and grimaced
    "this can't be right"
But I was too sweet to kick his ass
    "get away from me"
I managed a shrug to knock off
    his delinquent hand

Darlene C Alvarez

I sat hunched-back, as usual, on the foot
    of the bed
In my puffy gray and white parka
I had kept my cool but today I'm enraged

Isang puso

(Edited by M. Clar, K. Donahue & K. Cagampan)

Isusulat ko ito
Kahit hindi niya maiintindihan
Gusto kong sabihin
Hindi ko alam mag mahal
Na ka tulad nito
Kahit minsan

Magka-iba ang aming mukha
At magka-iba kami magsalita
Pero marunong siya magsabi
Sa akin "mahal na mahal kita"

Bakit ba hindi ako nag mahal
Nang kapwa ko – kasi nadala ako
Hindi ko matitiis kung
Iiwanan ako uli

Hindi niya maiintindihan ito
Kahit na sinulat ko
Hindi ko naman puedeng ilagay
Lahat ng nasa loob ng isang puso

It Is Time

This is about the time
I seek divine intervention
This is about the moment
I clasp my hands in prayer
This is about time.

This is about the time
I feel a metamorphosis commence
This is about the moment
I feel the twinge of nervousness
It is about time.

This is about time
That I'm squandering
Unbeknownst to me
Pointed out to me indirectly
But the message comes loud and clearly

This is about the time
I'm to make a life-altering decision

This is about the moment

I feel a twinge of apprehension

This is the right time.

This is the right time

I must write a new chapter

This is the right moment

I recognize what I'm going after

It is time.

It'll Be Better In A Second

To stop the rain
That would never end

So stubborn and so tough
Just broke 'cause he couldn't bend

To stop the pain
That would never mend

Irreversible and permanent
Maybe he should have thought it out
Than to be weak and succumb
To the unrelenting self-doubt

That welled up inside
Until it could flow no longer
You wonder what was so bad
That he couldn't deal and be stronger

But the deed is done

The feeble part won

Instead of letting nature take its course

Self-reliant, sure, but selfish, of course

Thought he was strong, but he was wrong

If only it were said

"it'll be better in a second" a second before he

Put a gun to his head

It's Not Me, It's You

You said any rainstorm we could pull through
Because our love will always be strong enough
Now it's raining buckets and you don't know
      what to do
I'm trying my best, but you've changed
Honey, it's not me, it's you

You said the boys before you didn't love me
They were only there to play me for a fool
You say I should be thankful because now
      I have you
You reassure me and tell me not to be insecure
Honey, it's not me, it's you

You say I don't know my history so
      Repeating it is my doom
Now I ask you about your past and conveniently
      You say I'm not sure

You say I'm a liar and that I'm holding back
    from you
Honey, it's not me, it's you

You say I have to change because the way I am
    could be better
Now I've taken your advice
Trying to be a perfect partner, too
But I see you're still not happy
Honey, it's not me, it's you

I Wish I Could Tell You

Don't hit your woman
because you've had too much to drink
Don't die one day
because you ate too many 'shrooms
so you decided to fly with the eagles you saw
Kiss your mother now and then
because you were her whole life

Joy To My World

(previously published in Shemom, 2005)

It took awhile to believe
there was a real human life in me
She was inside yet I felt enveloped
The warmth she created seeped
      through my pores
Creating what felt like an ethereal aura
That same glow is captured in her face
The shine encapsulated in her perfect
      pretty brown baby eyes
She turns to me with complete trust and faith
My icy heart dissolves as I speak
      "I hope I don't fail you."
The screams, cries, and wails were
      certainly of pain
More the emotional than the physical
As I am asked to present her to
And share her with the world

Krush

(Best Love Poem, The California Aggie Poetry Contest, 1995)

Your eyes peer deep into me

I do not understand

You have chosen these lips of mine

To fall victim to your charms

For your mere presence

Causes them to quiver

I think you noticed

I'm so embarrassed!

I do not understand

You hide a timid child

Behind a façade of coolness

Why must I see through that?

You made me feel attractive

Now I must blame you

From now on I will always hope

That you find me attractive

You silly goose

Forbidden feelings of fleeting passion

Envelop my being

Female

But you came running after me

Like in an old movie

Then I turned around

And you…you gave me

Your phone number!

Las Vegas Haiku (5)

Sin City it's called
Inhibition is unknown
All sorts of gaudy

Married by Elvis
Neon signs sizzle "I do"
Honeymoon away

Lady Luck's a bitch
Bright lights illuminating
Dreams of being rich

"Primm" and so proper
Outlets just a tram away
30-dollar rooms

Make sign of the cross
9 people in big red van
Safe trip, no drama

Last Warm Breeze of Summer

The last warm breeze of summer
    pushes its way
Through the cracked-open
    living room window
It cannot completely close - knob is broken.
I'm sitting on the daybed
Trying to keep from slipping
Sweetie is corralled between my legs
She beats on my thighs, like tribal drums
She shakes her head from left to right
    to the beat she's creating
Finally yelling out *ahhhhh*!
She twists her neck up and around as if to ask,
"Mama, did you hear how loud I can go?"
I say nothing.
Instead I smoothe her silky brown hair away
    from her forehead
Plant a little kiss
Reassured, she throws her arms up
Before dropping her body against mine

Like a rag doll

She turns her head to the left and as she turns

her gaze upwards to me

In goes her thumb into her tiny mouth

She suckles, suckles

Her eyes getting heavy

She delicately stokes my forearm, as she falls

    asleep

It felt as if a swatch of velvet brushed up

    against me

Softer than the last warm breeze of summer.

Looking Out Kleiber's Window

A swift and vicious wind
Rips through the late autumn skies
The branch of a sycamore tree
      Limps
Brown and dry leaves
Scurry along the pavement
Sounding like a brigade
Marching off to battle

Look, Ma, we're married

I said,

When we were kids

I used to wash your butt

I'm happy you've found

Someone special

To share your life with and

Who will wash your butt

When you're old and gray -

Happy wedding day!

Two years later…

He said,

The tears on your veil

Look like boogers!

We said,

Look, Ma, we're married

But not to each other!

Lover on Death Row

Like a prisoner my passions are caged

You have the key to release them

Like a guard, you have my freedom

Right there in your pocket

Hand it to me…

Instead I find a pack of cigarettes

And over a course of a few hours

I sucked on 20

But somehow I'm not satisfied…

I'd rather know that I'll never have you

Than to sit and stew and know you're

Within my reach, while I'm without

     a firm hold

I prefer the certainty of the execution table

Over this cell, which has slots of air

So I can breathe…

But my desire is suffocating me anyway

I'm either alone, or with you-

     not sometimes both!

Don't loiter around my door

I hear you turning the knob

Knowing darn well that I don't have

One on my side – to let you free me

For what you're doing to me

You should be on this side

But even if you tried it for a day

You would fail to comprehend

You would possess the benefit of knowing

It was not your true fate

I won't ask for much, but I implore you

Let us press ourselves against this wall

Between us

Allow the heat which emanates from only you

To melt away the icy skin

That's beginning to solidify…

Until I am granted clemency

Maybe it was decaf?

like
    pumping
        gas
            in
                a
                    junked
                        car
I
    drank
        some
            coffee
And
    I
        let
            out
                a
                    y a w n
As
    I
        gulped
            down
                the
                    last
                        drops

Montluçon, le 27-28 août 1995

Colored lights on a string

Parking lot, one car

Well-lit awning we were under

Man knocks over his glass of rosé

I avert my eyes

Charles stuffing his pockets with dinner rolls

Place mats: *il y a toujours une place pour les bons
vins à la table*

Very red grapes against a seedless-grape green
background

Au gratin crust

Charles finishing what I couldn't

Nos gestes de la politesse – invitations to our
homes

Glasses clinking "to the end of the workcamp."

His head aching from thinking too much in
English – 3-minute break

Bises x 3 from Mostafa of Morocco

Antonio, lighter and his broken pen

Hand on thigh middle-aged woman gets up

      from her seat
Philippe squatting
Aranxta not saying hi
Drinking alcohol – isopropyl flavor
Guard kicking us out – lights out (23h)
      -wait at the *quai*
Page d'écriture: Jacques Prévert
Relationships and Jean-Paul Sartre
Sophie patting Charles' butt adieu
Through the glass, watching Sophie and
      Mireille walk away
Dazed & Confused: a "call" from God
"Uncut" – a good job on Bobbitt
"we're sitting here and we're planning what
      we're going to see in Paris."
"I've never had so much fun waiting
      in a train station before."
"what does it feel like to be an American?"
"I'm happy to be your neighbor," he said.
No escalators.
2h30 train.

Musings of the Sunlight-Deprived

And though I should be suicidal
'cause it's the easy way out
Ultimately I realize it's cheaper, really
To live with the never-ending doubt

Do you ever get the ill feeling that
The life you live is not really your own
So even though you're there for so many
You feel isolated, cold and alone?

My Life as a Monk

(for C. Keller's class – 1988)

The sun has just set

The bell ringer is in the belfry

Ready to signal all the others that

A new day has come

But I usually get up

Before the chimes

I have vowed

A period of silence, celibacy and prayer

Since I cannot verbally express my thoughts

I write them in this journal that I keep

I am not allowed to talk to the others

My life is very quiet

Almost in silence

I live in a cell called a laura

We are required to wear brown robes

In the afternoon after lunch

I go to the school within the monastery
     to study

By sundown I return

To my laura and take a nap

I am usually awakened

By a monastery helper

Who brings me my supper

After which, I meditate for long hours

Until my mind, body and spirit get tired and

I fall asleep.

Another day of silence

Is ahead of me.

Oh When I Remember

Being serenaded by a string quartet
At the top of the marble stairs
Making sure not to cut the point off the brie
Choosing a wedge of lemon versus lime
In my sparkling water
Exchanging tales of Oratoire St. Joseph
In between bites of beef Wellington
Cascading wasa crisp crackers from the
Wicker cornucopia baskets
Wine flowing freely like the water
From the brass faucets I need only stick
    my hands under
When I got home my pinky was sore
Yet appearing unaffected was
    my only pretense
A kiss from an angel carrying a book
He said, "I'm a nerd!"
It was the coolest thing I'd ever heard…

Paper Dolls

His hand was neither rough nor soft

Neither warm nor cold

His dark and round eyes

Bore dark and round holes

In my memory

Fused together by a shake of our hands

Ephemeral and fleeting split-second

Forgotten as soon as the next one came

For a split-second, though

We even knew each other's name

It was ours unshared

Like the fibers in the fold

Joining paper dolls together

Our bond was as strong

Before it wafted away

Neither to never nor forever

Paris *encore*

kiss the lipstick marks off Oscar Wilde's
    marble
hum *light my fire* instead of *brown eyed girl*
    over Morrison's grave
recite prose to Molière and maybe make him
    laugh
secure silk scarves around my neck and
    handbag straps
hoard individually-wrapped pairs of rectangle
    sugar cubes
sip from my porcelain tasse
    freshly brewed café au lait UHT
eat imported Swiss cherries and nectarines
    even though cherries upset my stomach
make a wish and kiss my honey as we
sail on the Seine under Pont Alexandre III
shell out *beaucoup* for a
    shrimp cocktail from the *1er étage*
nibble as I scale the tower
recommend a hostel

to a Peruvian if he asks me

without paranoia, without annoyance

take the elevator to the *2ème étage*

picnic on Champs de Mars

tuna baguette

order fries for fun

with Ramazzotti blaring in the back

won't waste a minute writing a postcard

to a recipient who couldn't care less

they should be happy as me

oh, but I digress…

Maybe the gypsy girl will ask me for a handout

Maybe I will walk with her

Sans souci, it's Paris *encore*

Passenger

There was a free seat

In the reserved sideways section

So I took it

I'd shaved only up to the bottom of my knees

So I kept tugging at my pale-blue skirt

To cover the *Groucho* mustaches

Surely all eyes were on me

There was a seat

Close to the back door

So I sat by the window

It filled up fast and I had to share

With a stubby, greasy man

Whose stumpy ring and pinky fingers found

Their seat on my prepubescent left thigh

I just imagined his fingers were numb

Therefore, innocent and didn't diminish

    my own innocence

There was an aisle seat

On the already-crowded bus

With my back against the stranger

I just sat there

My feet dangling on the side

Obstructing traffic in the aisle

The bus used to go

Chug, chug, chug

As it slowed to a

                          Stop.

Peace o'Paper (POP)

Me, on the straight and narrow fell
In love and it made me swerve
For the longest they stepped on me
One day I threw them a curve

Who'd have thought
That I'd have the nerve
To get a restraining order
And have his ex served?

Can't she see truth will set her free
Like no bail bond can
Bitch - get a life
And get your own man!

Sure you could get him back
Then never have to contend with me
But what I've left on his soul and mind
Are marks I've made indelibly

Poke Her Face

Learn to be a poker face
Think a second before you react
Count 10 to 1 slowly before you speak

Jump off
Don't look first
Go ahead and look down
Told you it is worth it

Let your blood simmer
It's what it's there for
Not life if we needed to live on something
Maybe we could function only on
      Water
      Or coffee
      Or ice cream

I'm here and that's what I'm made of
I need a drink
A kick in the ass

A blast of color

A slap in the face

I need you to poke me in my face

Check for any vital signs

I hate to need you so much.

Preservation

Surely the dead man's body
Relishes how the ridges in
Her fingertip comb the superfine hairs
On his cinnamon skin
Misses the supple, malleable flesh
Through which you can hear
The gentle hum of warm crimson blood
As it voyages through the intricate network
That runs the length
Recalls the uncomfortable yet pleasing
Sensation of
Uncontrollable fluids spilling
The condensation from the heat of bodies
(in constant motion)
Spontaneous, deliberate, improvisation
Remembers clothed in nothing but
Otherworldly elements
He's now one with
Sadly, only physically
Mourns his inability to seemingly float

With feet firmly planted

Filling his lungs

With a substance

He has never seen before

But unconditionally trust

Will sustain him

      The feeling

      The network

      The process

      The sensation.

Prière du chat

(for S. Clay's class – 1993)

Mon Dieu, Vous m'avez crée

Très méchant

Mais, il me semble que les gens

M'aiment de toute façon.

Je pense que je ne mérite pas

De m'en sortir avec tout ce que je fais

Je suis petit, mais je suis puissant

Je pense qu'il est impossible d'être les deux.

Ce n'est pas de ma faute

Que les enfants me prennent pour un jouet.

Si je n'étais pas comme çela:

Mignon et petit

Je serais respecté

Puisque je suis crée ainsi:

Mignon et petit

Les enfants jouent avec moi.

Aujourd'hui, j'ai entendu

Un garçon qui a dit

"Qu'il est doux!"

J'étais fâché.

Personne n'a jamais dit

A mes cousins, les lions:

"Qu'ils sont mignons!"

Mon Dieu, je Vous demande

Que Vous me fassiez respectable!

Ainsi soit-il.

Puedo amar

Puedo llenar

Su cuerpo

Con todo mi amor

Puedo poner

En su memoria

Una imagen de mi flor

Puedo llevarle

En su boca

Un poco de mi sabor

Puedo abrir

Su camino cerrado

Cuando este muy cansado

Quiero dormir ahora

(Edited by J. Alvarez)

Quiero dormir ahora,
Porque tengo sueño.
Al pensar sobre el amor
      me en tristeze
No se porque.

Quiero estar alegre denuevo.
Pero necesito calmarme.
Con dolor en mis ojos
Estoy dispuesta hablar con el.

Estoy dispuesta hablar con el
Con dolor en mis ojos.
Pero necesito calmarme.
Quiero estar alegre denuevo.

No se porque
      me en tristeze
Al pensar en el amor.
¿Por que tengo sueño?
Quiero dormir.

Red-Light Runner

Look how hot I am
They call when they need
A diversion

Look how desirable I am
They call when they need
Their manhood regenerated

Look how sad I am
When I call, they're not around

Look how cold they are
When they don't consider
My true worth

Look how blind I am
To think I'm worth
This substandard treatment

Look how weak I am

As I run to answer the phone

Oops, I'm not fast enough

Machine's picked up another sweet come-on

Another unoriginal manipulation

Look how easy I am

My heart swoons

I think "he's the one."

While I doodle my new last name

Look how pathetic I am

Returning the call

Sure enough it's an innocent invite

Which I accept knowing…

Look how strong I'll be

Sweetly refusing

Then asking to be taken home

To my answering machine

The flashing light seems to announce:

"Look how wanted I am."

Darlene C Alvarez

When really I should see the light

For what it is: a flashing red one.

Roller Skates

I was 4 inches taller
standing in my white,
lace-up roller skates.
It had cherry-red
wheels and a pink stopper,
like an overgrown pencil eraser.

I rolled down the hill
along Appleton Avenue…
Tracy lived on the Highland Avenue side
She opened the door wearing
only her stinky pinky panties
The kind with the polyester crotch, probably

As I entered, I could hear
controversy blaring
from the record player
Tracy started dancing and
singing, "Punch your pussy…"

She was nasty -

covering her sticky kitchen floor

in a rainbow of colors with

crinkled cupcake baking liners.

We filled each one with a chocolate treat then

ate them in Tracy's gray and damp bedroom

where the walls were covered with yellowing

newspaper - comic strips, actually

Tracy insisted, "you're supposed to

      close your eyes!"

Routine

I get up every morning reluctantly painfully
I curse this blasted routine that rules me
But I forget to thank God for letting me stay
    today

I make some coffee and stir in the sugar
Who put the empty carton of creamer back
    in there?
I forget about the little boy who has to walk
    half a mile
To fetch a bucket of water

I put on my perfectly coordinated outfit
Seems the dryer ate my last pair of socks
But I forget the little girl risking shards
As she makes her way to the corner store

I sprint to catch my bus before he closes
    the door
Standing, I roll my eyes as I ride with my face

Pressed again the windshield
But I forget the little boy walking to school
      before dawn, fearing ghosts

At the end of the day, I get ready for bed
Dreading the routine which waits for me
      in the morning
But I remember to thank God
For this comfortable monotony

Salope ivrée

Je n'étais pas sûre

Si je voulais lui embrasser doucement

Avec la tendresse comme

Ce qu'une mère sent pour son enfant…

Ou si je voulais étouffer son être

Avec une passion brûlante

Réservé exclusivement

D'habitude pour mon vrai amant.

Settling

Like dust on objects still and barely living
Like a nomad, for just a while
Like the fruit at the bottom of un-pre-stirred
      yogurt
Like cereal, after its 14-hour voyage to the store
Like a newbie anywhere
Like dating another because the one you want
      asked your friend out instead
Like getting a car the bank says you can only
      afford
Like dating a flake of a man for some
      semblance of a relationship

This passive pattern is safe

But a call to chaos again
Is the sound my drummer's making

Silent Lamb

It would be nice to know that I'm no weakling
I don't want to be a nice guy all the time
I want to finish first sometimes, too

So I remain in my demure cage
Raging emotions boiling contained

To borrow a friend's phrase,
"I seem to have my act together on the
      outside."
Composure alone seems to subliminally
      command respect
So I try to be nice
Then…
      Squish!

Split Ends

Why try to make ends meet
Then wish for a fork in the road
The struggle justifies your existence
It's as if you're nobody
Unless you've got a hefty load

On your shoulders
That weighs you down
And makes you slump
Day to day living is predicated upon
You getting over that monstrous hump

Lest your idle body becomes the
Devil's workshop
Something's gotta keep you going
Heaven forbid you slow down
And actually have time to stop!

Why try to make ends meet
When it's so much more fun

To split them

For we know that if we had

More time or money

We'd be at a loss as to

What to do with them…

Spoiled

You made me feel worthy of so much

I've never had before

I was content with just enough or a little

Yet unsatisfied when that's what I got

Not until you came along

Did I appreciate

The pleasures of a little more

Step

Why should she call the child "stepson"
So they will see.
So they will see?
Her grace
Her accepting, unconditional embrace

Why should he call the new wife "stepmother"
So they will see.
So they will see?
His scorn
His family inexplicably torn

Who is this stranger
Taking my father, to whom I assign blame?

I am this stranger
Who has even assumed your last name

Still Questioning

No need to prove it any further
I am not mentally sound
But I mean this non-pejoratively speaking
Oh! Joyous facetiousness
I dream of a sanctuary
No time to go anywhere real
I bask in my drunken stupor instead
At least now I'm closer to home
I felt I used to be strewn everywhere
I carried on with no focus, just scattered
My mind out of town like a dreamer
Sometimes I wonder what goes on in others'
      minds
I need that validation that I'm not alone
What drives others to do what they do?
Could it be they wonder, too?
I want to be independent and yet, belong
Or is that an oxymoronic phrase
Like, "apathetically masturbating"?
I want to be one of a kind

You know, like everyone else

Suspend-Her

Since I feel suspended, I'm

Searching for a goal to anchor me

Like the ropes on balloons in the

Thanksgiving Day Parade

Until I long to break free from it – again

And when I'm free

I'll be uneasy because

Flying is not natural to me

Then I will seek solid ground of steel

In case I want to bounce back

Because my sneakers are rubber-soled

And can only take me so far.

Synthetic Happy Place

Vicodin coursing through my veins
Brings me to my happy place
I'm suspended in air, painless
Like a drop of oil in a water vase

Alcohol marinating my insides
Brings me to a tingly place
I transcend the ugly, I'm numb
Like my legs after a marathon race

White-out wafting up my nostrils
Brings me to a higher place
I block out the bad, see only good
Like my mistakes magically erased

Nicotine floating in my lungs
Brings me to a calmer place
I lower my blood pressure, lose weight
Like a diet pill with better taste

Lovin' happening in the room

Brings me to a soothing place

I undulate from the inside out

Like a baritone projecting the bass…

Take Back The Wheel

The gas tank empties

With each mile I go

There's still quite a-ways to go

There will be no

Refilling station along the way

That's what I get

For taking the scenic route

It's the price I've had to pay

Chasing the sun is such a tasking venture

It's the purpose of my days

Its rays guide me and

At the same time push me away

This rolling stone has turned into a huge
        moss ball

Its weight acts like brakes I did not apply

Against my will, I surrendered my wheel

But I'm taking it back!

No use crying over wasted gas

I've still got quite a-ways to go

Taken For Granted

I turn green whenever she flips her hair
My stomach turns when she touches your arm
My blood boils when she laughs at everything
    you say
What does she want? She wants you.
And you like that.

I turn red whenever you enjoy such attention
My mouth frowns when you entertain her
My butt wrinkles when your eyes glaze over
    her face
What do you want? You want her.
I don't feel good.

I turn blue whenever you are out of sight
My eyes shift left and right to the beat of worry
My heart sinks when you don't pick up when
    I call
What do I want? My self-esteem
I'm feeling better now.

I turn **pink** whenever he waves to me from
      across the way
My chest heaves when he smiles the way
      he does
My heart flutters when he says my French is
      really good
What do I want? I want him.
I like this.

I turn **white** as I find you at my doorstep
My hands sweat as I play back my
      mental affair
My brow arches as I wonder what brings
      you here
What do you want? You want me.
I don't get this.

I turn **black & blue** in the places you stepped
      all over
My face turns hard as I begin to lose my faith
My eyes lower as I let you take me for granted

What do I want? Respect and appreciation.
I really deserve it.

Tea Leaves

When I'm raging inside and boiling
I bubble till I'm spent
Reading the residue like tea leaves
I decide today that it spells 'unconfident'

The Carousel (bittersweet '01)

I was singing my country song

When he pulled the plug on my amp

Told me I was living all wrong –

He lit up a kerosene lamp

Then he held it up to my face

Told me to take a long hard look

Said it was such a disgrace

Looking at all the things they took:

My home, my dad – ain't it sad?

My job at a dead-end, can't find a single friend

Who's worth the title; I was like an engine left
       to idle

I was singing my blues-y song

When he pulled up a chair to lean in closer

Told me I wouldn't do this for long

"You're getting off that roller coaster!"

He offered his hand to lead me on
The carousel of horses and a sleigh
Then promised from this point on
We would be happy living this way

Occasional ups and downs
Surrounded by beauty 360 degrees
In our love we'd always be home
As long as our hearts were holding the keys.

The Collector

Is it genius

Is it a disorder

It is both

And neither one

Someone tell them

You can't take it with you

What you collect

Takes you

The clock man

Made the news again

"fall back"

Begging for sympathy for his plight

Having to wind all 853 clocks

Collected over his lifetime

And counting…

As if more clocks meant more time

To spend, to waste, to collect

It is genius

It is a disorder

With no cure for either.

The Love Dispenser

The dating game is a lot like
using the vending machine.
You think you're making the selection,
when really your options are choosing you.
You may have a countless amount
from which to choose
but you only really have access
to what is immediately in front of you.

OK. So you're in front of
the vending machine.
You want those salty pretzels
about 6 rows back, but you can't get them
until you go past the nutty candy bars and
sour gummies in front of it.
Then you think to yourself,
"Hmmm, how badly do I want those pretzels?"
You either make an alternate selection, like,
"I'll take the granola bar for now"
or you simply, walk away.

Maybe you decide to return later to try again.
Maybe the pretzels you wanted are now right
there, front and center.

If it's meant to be, you make your selection and
it slowly advances toward you.
It'll literally fall into your hands and there –
you have found each other.

On the other hand, if the fates dictate
otherwise, your selection does not complete
the "advance" and it does not fall to your, um,
feet. It is stuck. You are stuck.
What do you do?

With clenched fists, you bang
on the glass with all your might.
"Come to me. I want to make you mine!"

Now if you're really persistent,
you start shaking the machine.

It starts to shift and slip and collapse
on top of you.
You decide some things are worth the risk.

And so it is with love.
The lengths that some, you and I, will go to
in order to obtain the one we want!

Let's say you don't go that direction.
You don't get your pretzels.
So you ask for a refund.

This represents a second chance.

You take a chance. Maybe.

Or you walk away.

And return…

Then and Now
(previously published in Teen-Age Magazine, 1990)

Click,
I turn the TV on
Lives taken have risen
To more than 1,000
The newsman says.

I ask, "How could that be? There is no war."

Why then, do the aircrafts
Just fall out from the sky?
Were they just flying too high?

Mr. President, I ask you
"Did you make a hole-in-one?
While you send thousands of our people
And watch…
And hope to say, "We won."

The city council calls a meeting
We hear, "Beautify the neighborhoods."

The workers hear, "Clean up the bloody
> sidewalks…
And sweep away the shells."

Mr. Baseball player hits a homer
A couple million all the way to the bank
Ms. Education molds minds of the future
A bronze plaque hangs on the wall

A child of six
Pays fare of three quarters and a dime
While I, adult,
Pay the same for mine

I won't close my eyes
And pretend they aren't there
Someday I'll ask,
"Where's war?"
And they'll say, "Nowhere."
Someday. Somewhere.

The Sister I Never Had

By being my friend today
You cannot be the you who never:

Lived in the projects, across the way from me
Spent the night at my place when your mother
    ran off with her boyfriend, again
Ate instant noodles for days on end
Wore MJ *thriller* earrings
Sang *la isla bonita* with me from start to finish,
    acapella
Watched TV game shows over the phone
    with me while you were in the hospital
    for 3 days with meningitis

I'll think of you each December 9
Every time I see an Elvis poster
Each time I hear *this used to be my playground*
I miss you, but I'll let you go
So you are free to be who you are today
I was blessed to know a beautiful you

Ages ago

I miss you, but I'll let you go

The Slumber He Seeks

The slumber he seeks

Is satisfied there

For this while, he is in my possession

His body, heart and the dreams

Undulating in his mind are

Here with me

This brings me security and comfort

As I don't have a single question to ask

I'm all at once filled with contentment

Tongue alive

New Zealand mussels, harvested

last December

Iridescent half-shell

Roasted-garlic rice vinegar –

My brain thinking *adobo*

Finely-chopped cilantro –

My brain thinking "salsa for chips"

Fresh-squeezed lemon juice –

Ah, yes, my senses come alive!

Coarsely-ground salt on the tongue

Makes it feel fresh from the shore

Better slurped to satisfaction

Too Much on my Template

My guy lavishes his luscious lips on me
Like he loves me
Feeds me with his thick fingers and
We drink from the same glass
Rubs his nose on my erogenous neck
Craves only food and music
More than me
Fun-loving, carefree
Risk-taking, hygienic
Calls twice a week, not smothering
Strolling naked on the beach at night
Or in the living room in light
Drinks socially
Philosophizes…
Because he's all this and more,
He's handsome and sexy
Simply delectable!

Can't wait for his expression
The first time I meet him

Tough As Nails

I'm painting my nails, however
Not to strengthen them
But rather, to toughen up myself
Not quite tough as nails right now…
I paint my nails a shade of rose
To remind myself of the calm person within
She is always patient, calm and collected
      But today I lost it!
So I paint my nails
      they now shine prettily rose
Like petals on a blooming bouquet
With its opening there comes forth
A new beginning
      so it is with patience
She gave herself time to close
Yet develop internally
      open once again anew and
Alive – more strong, shiny
More resilient.

Trust me, sweetie

Look what you made me do

Renewed my faith

Restored my hope

Forgiven my enemies

      And my friends

Banished my cynicism

Melted my heart

Revitalized my ailing spirit

Rejuvenated my ancient soul

Refocused my view

I only see ahead

We are embarking on an amazing journey

Trust me, sweetie.

Two Words

pamplemousse

potential

-words I love and hate

respectively

round, yellow citrus

pucker-inducing

self-elevating back-handed

pat on the back

respectfully

Une amie qui s'appelait Rose

(for J. Wagnild's class – 1992)

«Je vois la vie en rose...»

Quelqu'un a chanté

Je chanterai aussi

«Je vis la vie d'une rose...»

Je danserai dans l'eau du matin

J'y serai pour vous

Vous pouvez me donner

A vos amies et à votre femme

Vous pouvez m'offrir à elles

Vous vous êtes disputés?

Donnez-moi à cette personne

Et elle vous pardonnera

Etes-vous malade?

Je suis la meilleure médecine.

Rêvez-vous? Respirez-moi.

Je suis réelle.

Quand vous étiez triste, j'étais là

Quand vous pleuriez, je recevais

Vos larmes - l'eau de vos yeux

Une, deux, trois

Sur mes bras

Je pensais que c'était

L'eau du matin

Alors, je commençais à danser

Vous souriiez

Vous n'étiez plus triste

Et puis, vous avez découvert

Qu'elle vous adorait encore.

Alors, vous avez continué votre

Liaison amoureuse…

Pendant que moi, je dansais

Dans mes larmes…

L'eau de mes yeux pour vous.

Je me demande,

«Est-ce que c'est la vie d'une rose?»

Unsentimental

Let me take you for granted
You're just in my neighborhood
You'll remain unacknowledged
Until you say you're leaving for good

I figured you'd always be there
That I could call you "next time"
Now that you're leaving, I say,
"when you're in town, drop me a line"

These are things we say to someone going
     away
Albeit a little too late
"write me, call me, let's keep in touch"
When before I didn't care all that much

Because if I did this would be much harder for
     me
But I find it's easy to bid you adieu
You could have reached out, y'know

Uh, hello, it goes both ways, where were you,
    too?

Ironically, the farther you are, the closer
    we'll be
The difference will be the effort we'll make
It always takes someone's departure to see
    they were right here
Now we'll only have to deal with each other
    a couple times a year…

Valentine

You have touched my soul

Without saying

A word…and have

Allowed me

To realize

The person within

And all it took

Was just…one look

Into those

Pretty brown eyes

Walking Around Squinting

I see how you shield me from
Their fascinated stares
I know you are not ashamed of me
We spend time in public places
Yet the insecure adolescent in me
Asks in paranoia, "what are they thinking?"
Their eyes shift back and forth, from you to me

Would your stares try to burn
Like the crosses in your backyards
I see something in your eye
It's a white thread
I understand you now
My view would be limited, too
If I had to walk around squinting

Who askew?

Rather than being safe and logical
And ask where that dick has been
You cross yourself and pray to saints
And ask, "am I committing a sin?"

Rather than worrying about disease
That can harm or ultimately take your life
You worry and fret over getting knocked-up
Without first becoming somebody's wife

Rather than seeing how this behavior
Can forever alter your attitude
Toward having sex in the context of love
You're hurt he didn't call – how rude!

Rather than listening to your goody-goody friends
Who tell you to slow the hell down
You're furious with them 'cause now it means
     you'll have to find
Your own way to the club downtown…

Winner

What once eluded me
Is now within my grasp
I'm finishing first now
Not second to last

I pump both arms in victory
Leading the pack - who would've guessed
Triumphant – my hard work paid off
Now they're rewarding my best

When you reach the glorious summit
They say there's not a single sound
Just the pounding of your heart that got you
    here
With the clouds all around

Wisdom

I've walked through the force field of that
      emotion
And have blaze marks gained from re-entry

The experience may replicate itself
But this one will never be again

I'm different from yesterday, tomorrow
      = change
Hopefully, I'm a superlative!

Own my impulses and my pragmatism
Shine brilliantly like a flawed prism.

You Said To Me

"Don't be so hard on yourself."
You said to me.
"Things will look up,
Just wait and see.

Times get tough
I know they do.
Put a smile on your face,
Don't look so blue.

A tear is forming
In your eye
Look at me and
Don't you cry.

I'm here for you
I'll always be
I will listen when
You talk to me."

I look in your eyes
Somehow I'm less sad
This is the best talk
That I've ever had.

For you looked at me
And held my hand tight
The three words you said
Made everything right.

"Things will look up,
Just wait and see.
I love you."
You said to me.

You think?

One would think
      a man with sisters
would treat women splendidly

One would think
      an educated person
would always do the smart thing

One would think
      an elderly person
would be wise and mature

One would think
      a church-going girl
would be chaste

One would think
      the lottery winner
would never again know debt

The Quiet Child

One would think
> Women, since we all have vaginas

would not be bitches toward one another

One would think
> the meek and the stupid

would do no harm

One would think
> your fellow-countryman

would have your back

One would think
> she's happy and sweet because she

smiled
> you think she is the quiet child

www.ingramcontent.com/pod-product-compliance
Lightning Source LLC
Chambersburg PA
CBHW051801040426
42446CB00007B/454